CAREER AS A
CARTOON ARTIST
ANIMATOR

ANIMATORS AND CARTOONISTS DRAW on their talents every day, bringing colorful characters to life in a world where anything is possible. If you really love drawing, have a vivid imagination, a continuous flow of ideas, a tireless creative streak, and a willingness to work hard, you just might want to pencil yourself in for a career in animation and cartooning.

Interestingly, a great deal of animation and cartooning is steeped in reality. Artists who create the best cartoon characters are those who can draw lifelike people and animals that seem to jump off a page or out of a movie screen. The characters appear ready to walk right into a viewer's life.

How does an artist accomplish this? By having an eye for detail. These insightful cartoonists study the shape, size, and structure of the human body, as well as the bodies of animals, birds, and all living creatures that they might one day want to capture on the drawing board. In their minds, top animators and cartoonists have recorded thousands of human gestures, reactions, and expressions. They are keenly aware of the way people and animals move. Add to that, meticulous observations about the forms of endless objects around us, and you have the makings of magical creations of a surreal world where animals talk, plants cry, trees move, candlesticks give advice, and people fall off cliffs, get run over by steamrollers, and fall out of airplanes – only to live to tell the tale.

This ability to draw reality precisely allows an artist to start distorting that drawing, contributing twists and turns, and blends of fantasy that seem perfectly plausible to the viewer. Elongated heads, stubby legs, pronounced wide-rimmed glasses, strange walks, and peculiar postures – all spring from the imagination of inventive animators and cartoonists as they give their characters distinctive physical attributes that will make them stand out and become memorable. They add movements, actions, and voices done by experienced actors who express the personalities of characters just as the artists envisioned them when these drawings started out as simple circles, triangles, and lines on a sketchpad. The test of an animator is to be able to draw a character that conveys feeling and emotion to an audience.

A challenging career with limitless possibilities, the field of animation art requires you to be willing to start at the bottom and work your way up. This could mean years of developing someone else's ideas and concepts before you get a chance to show what you can do on your own. On the other hand, this field is growing so rapidly that there is a chance you can get your breakout assignment sooner rather than later, as artists with a fresh view are sought to create innovative work for multiple media, from magazines to computer games, comic books to commercials, animated television shows to major motion pictures.

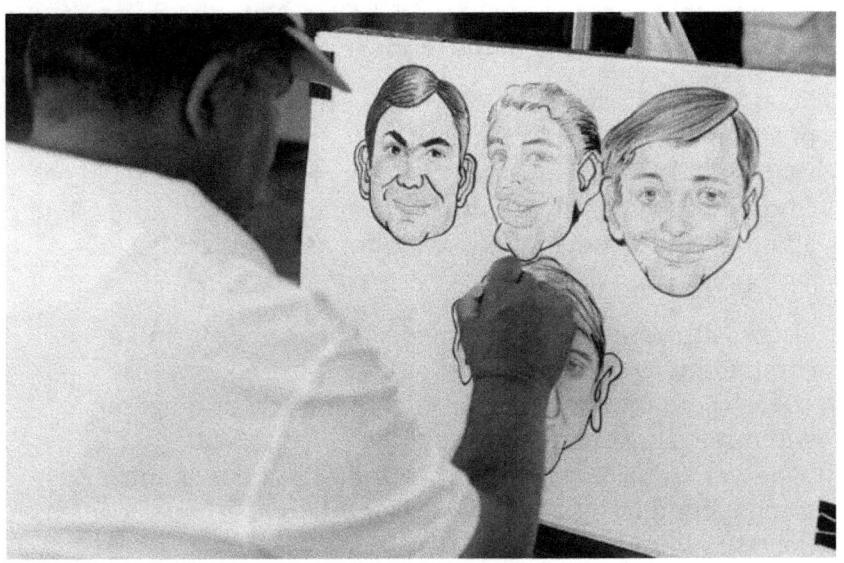

WHAT YOU CAN DO NOW

DRAW, DRAW, AND DRAW SOME MORE. This is one field where practice really does make perfect, and constantly drawing certainly helps an artist truly evolve. You need to keep improving your skills and sharpening your technique.

Many up-and-coming cartoonists and animators spend hours watching people in public places, like parks and shopping centers, and drawing what they see. They learn something from every drawing they do. They often capture people making the transition from one movement to another, changing facial expressions, and making an array of gestures.

Study cartoons in newspapers, magazines, comic books, advertisements, even board games – anywhere you see illustrated work. Watch as many television cartoons and animated films as you have time to, looking for insights and pointers that can make your work better. Note the different styles and the diversity in the work.

Read as much as you can about drawing. There are many excellent how-to books for both cartoonists and animators that teach the fundamentals necessary to excel in the field. Find out if there is an art school or community center near you that offers courses in drawing for aspiring young cartoonists.

Check with your school newspaper and yearbook, and a community newspaper as well, to see if the editors will publish your work. Be willing to contribute your drawings without fee, just to get the published credit. Brush up on your writing skills, too – many cartoonists and animators do some writing to go along with their artwork, especially when they draw comic strips.

HISTORY OF THE CAREER

HOW FAR BACK DOES CARTOONING go? One could argue that it dates back to prehistoric times because of archaeological finds of crude, cartoon-like drawings on the walls of cave dwellers.

Caricatures have even been found in comic strip-type layouts in ancient Egyptian pyramids. That certainly shows an early love for drawing that still thrives to this day.

The history of cartoons has always centered on humor and satire. Noted British artist and printmaker William Hogarth (1697–1764) often took breaks from the seriousness of his realistic portraiture to grab his sketchpad and draw a stinging commentary on some of the hot-button moral and political issues of his day. His drawings were complete with written observations and done in a row of sequential frames that is now recognized as the format for comic strips. Hogarth's ability to get to the core of the question with his insightful artwork and biting words, made his drawings an effective method to express his opinions about politics and society.

Soon, others were encouraged to use the same medium to poke fun at the gaffes made by the rich and powerful, and spotlight many of society's shortcomings. The work of British cartoonist Thomas Rowlandson (1756 – 1827) benefitted greatly from the rapid rise in newspaper distribution. His relentless attacks on moral decadence gave those in the poorer classes hope that someone was on their side, calling attention, with a glib satirical twist, to the injustices that so many in the upper echelons callously ignored.

British caricaturist George Cruikshank (1792 – 1878) hammered away at political corruption as well as the shortcomings of England's Industrial Revolution in his drawings, making him a hero of the downtrodden and an enemy of industrialists and landowners. Other European artists, like Honoré Daumier of France (1808 – 1879) and Spain's Francisco Goya (1746 – 1828) used cartoons to pointedly expose inequalities and malfeasance in their nations.

Political cartoons were part of the culture in colonial America in the mid-1700s, especially in the years leading up to the American Revolution. The British Parliament was a constant target for colonial cartoonists, as was England's King George III.

Once the colonies won their independence from England, with freedom of the press as one of the foundations of the US Constitution, cartoons lampooning politicians showed no signs of letting up. Public figures were lampooned by newspapers with an artist and a viewpoint.

Thomas Nast (1840 – 1902) had one of the biggest impacts on political cartoons in the United States, creating many caricatures that are still with us today, including the symbols of the Republican Party (the elephant), the Democratic Party (the donkey), and Uncle Sam.

By the 1870s, the United States starting seeing its first wave of cartoonists whose work was purely humorous, poking fun at everyday life but not necessarily having a political slant. Some of this work was carried regularly in popular magazines. But most of these comical views of life appeared in Sunday newspapers and laid the groundwork for the American tradition of the Sunday funnies.

By the 1920s, magazines like the New Yorker started featuring an ironic, more sarcastic style of humor in its cartoons. Comic books first appeared in the United States in 1933, launching many opportunities for cartoonists. The first comic books contained reprints of an array of Sunday comic strips; hence the term "comic books." Since their introduction, comic books have covered all kinds of subjects, from comedy to fantasy to drama to science fiction and action heroes.

While cartooning continued to flourish in the print media, it also found a place very early in the film industry. The first animated cartoon short silent film was made in 1906 by newspaper cartoonist turned filmmaker J. S. Blackton. Between 1906 and the end of the silent film era in 1929, many newspaper comic strips were turned into short silent films. The enormous amount of work that went into creating an animated film during the silent-movie era limited how many could be produced. Gradually, technical advances – including the process of drawing directly on celluloid – made animated moviemaking easier and more cost-effective.

In 1923, Walt and Roy Disney founded their cartoon studio. Walt Disney introduced Mickey Mouse in 1928, a character that met with instance success. Disney helped make many of the advances in animation with sound, color, and, in 1937, the epic feature-length movie *Snow White and the Seven Dwarfs*. *Snow White* was just the first of a number of Disney animated feature-length hit movies in the 1940s, '50s, and

'60s.

Other studios specializing in animation began to spring up in the mid-20th century, creating full-length movies, and, with the growing popularity of television in the 1950s, animated cartoons for the small screen as well.

In the 1970s, animated films slumped; the public seemed to lose interest in them. Many studios that made animated films were forced to close down. In the late 1980s, however, animated films began to rebound, led by Disney Studios with films like *The Little Mermaid* (1989). The market has been strong ever since, including expansion into 3-D. Animation has also played a major role in the success of computer games.

WHERE YOU WILL WORK

SINCE MOST ANIMATORS WORK IN teams, they usually have offices together within film studios. In these surroundings, it is easy for everyone to get together informally to discuss ideas and look at each other's work to see how a project is progressing.

There are large animation companies, like Disney and Pixar, and smaller companies as well. Some companies work on feature-length films and popular television shows, while others are involved in smaller projects, like short cartoons and commercials.

Cartoonists can work in a number of places, including at home. Big comic book publishers, like filmmaking companies, have studios where teams of artists and writers work together. There is always plenty of room in these studio settings for brainstorming sessions to take place. During these meetings, drawings can be spread out, ideas can be exchanged and fleshed out, and artists can do long-term planning for each title, drawing on the insights of everyone who is responsible for getting these comics out to eager fans.

Political cartoonists often set up shop in a newspaper office, where they are surrounded by all the late-breaking news that helps make their work timely and relevant. Cartoonists who work for a magazine can usually find a place for their drawing boards in the publication's office. By being on site, artists can see what articles are going in the next issue and coordinate their artwork. Some cartoonists do specific drawings to go along with particular stories, and being on site gives them an idea about how an editor is planning to lay out the article and the artwork needed to accompany it.

Advertising agencies are another place cartoonists are likely to be employed. These artists draw the storyboards for TV commercials, as well as create characters and drawings for ad campaigns.

Book publishers, especially those with a children's division, always have a staff of creative cartoonists in house. Books for young children must be enhanced with eye-catching, colorful, fun illustrations. Books for older children need attention-grabbing cover art.

Many book-publishing companies put out calendars and some of them are hand-drawn. So you just might find yourself, sketchbook in hand, surrounded by a bunch of manuscripts that need illustration.

Working in the offices of a greeting card company is another setting many cartoonists find well suited to their talents. In this environment, not only will cartoonists illustrate cards containing greetings created by staff and freelance writers, but they will get the chance to draw cover and inside art for cards with greetings they write themselves.

There is also freelance work. Many freelancers get steady work from publications that use their drawings on a regular basis. Others turn to newspapers, magazines, book publishers, and greeting card companies that hire outside contractors to take on work during busy seasons. You will have to set up a studio in a quiet area of your home, but you can't beat the convenience.

JOBS FOR CARTOONISTS

THERE'S TRUTH TO THE SAYING, "A picture is worth a thousand words." For cartoonists, it's the picture you draw that conveys the meaning. The job is about developing drawings with characters and themes that viewers will respond to.

Political Cartoonists

Cartoonists work in a variety of fields. For political cartoonists, current events are the driving force behind their work, which is published in newspapers, magazines, and websites. You need to have your finger on the pulse of news, even anticipating events before they happen. Single cartoons usually appear on a daily basis and focus on an event or personage in the news.

The work of political cartoonists reflects the times we live in. Like reporters, some political cartoonists cover world events, and others national issues, while state and local themes are the inspiration behind the drawings in regional and community publications. You have to know the subject well enough to express through your drawings what people are thinking, the essence of the issue or event. You have to strike a common chord.

Some cartoonists are known for the personal slant they put on an issue. Others play it solely for the humor or the irony inherent in a topic. You establish that relationship with readers. It's what keeps them coming back. Some readers will love your point of view. Others will hate it, but you express it so well, so knowledgeably, and so many people talk about your work, that even your detractors do not want to miss it.

Each day's work builds on the last. You are deciphering the news in pictures, not in words. You have to be relevant. You have to be timely. You have to be the person with the idea for the cartoon that makes everyone say, "I wish I had thought of that."

Not every cartoonist likes the fast pace of daily newspapers and 24/7 websites. Some like to submit work for magazines on a weekly or monthly basis, or supply drawings to websites on an occasional basis. These cartoons must still reflect current themes and trends, but the artist can take a bit more time with them. The ideas do not have to come as quickly, but they have to be as sharp and crisp.

In magazines like *The New Yorker,* people have come to expect cartoons that are literate, insightful, and clever. In these magazines, cartoonists are expected to pick up on what most people are thinking about, and illustrate it. You need to have a keen insight into the experiences of ordinary people and their relevant attitudes. You might draw a frustrated customer at a self-service checkout wondering how all this automation makes life easier when the darn thing just won't work!

Comic Strips

Newspapers and some magazines also publish comic strips. These comic strips are usually sold to the publication through a news service called a syndicate. The same syndicated comic strip may appear in hundreds of outlets on one day. The theme of a comic strip can be serious or humorous, sometimes cute or even silly. Your major task is to develop a character or group of characters that people care about and want to follow every week or several days a week.

The Peanuts comic strip is a good example. People can relate to the characters who run into the same problems they run into every day. They say things people in those same situations wish they could think of. Your readers suffer along with the characters, and they laugh with them as well. Your characters become friends of your readers. Readers look forward to seeing these characters in the pages of their local newspaper. They want to find out what is going on in the lives of these characters, how they solve problems, and how they find humor in adversity.

You must be able to draw people into your work. You want your comic strip to be one of the reasons people buy the newspaper. Keeping the comic strip fresh, lively, and pertinent is both a challenge, and what you love about the work.

Comic strips allow people to engage their imagination. That gives you the leeway to do the absurd, like giving inanimate objects thoughts and personalities. You can let people peer into a fantasy world you created, and they can join in the fun.

Comic Books

If you have a yen for adventure, you might find your way into the world of comic books. Not every comic book revolves around super heroes, but that seems to be the most popular format today. If you get a job with an existing comic book, you will have to stay true to the theme of the book, the storyline, the drawing style, and the continuing characters.

If you are lucky enough to be in on the creation of a new comic book, you will have more creative freedom. Once you set the tone for the book and characters, you have to stick with it. As with most cartooning, you have to keep the work exciting and current. You have to know what comic book fans are looking for in their characters and you have to deliver that.

While comic books need a catchy storyline, in the end the artwork is what really grabs the fans. Therefore, the pressure is on you to deliver, issue after issue. Staying up-to-date with the competition is part of your job. It is not enough in the comic book business to be as good as the competition. You have to be better, and that usually means your artwork has to be very inventive and well drawn. Comic book fans have a keen eye. They know when the artwork is slipping, when it is getting tired or sloppy. The fans want you to keep pushing the envelope. Comic book artists are tested as much as the super heroes they draw.

Greeting Cards

It may not seem as challenging as creating a comic book, but imagine coming up with new drawings for Mother's Day cards or Valentine's cards every year. Fresh ideas are what keep greeting card companies on top in their business. The companies turn to cartoonists for those ideas. What makes someone pick up one card off the rack instead of another? Usually it is an eye-popping drawing. People are looking for something new, something they have not seen in a card before. That is what the cartoonist brings – that irresistible drawing that makes one greeting card company's Valentine's card a trendsetter.

Children's Books

Many cartoonists put their talents to work illustrating children's books. This requires you to use your imagination, and know what would appeal to and intrigue children. Coming up with funny-looking characters, vibrant colors, wild shapes, and graphics arranged in a way that would make a child want to read the book again and again – that is your challenge. The work starts with reading the manuscript and then putting together some rough ideas for the illustrations.

Next, you map out the book, with your drawings surrounded by the narrative. Once your rough drawings are approved, you get to work on refining the illustrations, and then finally submit the finished product.

ANIMATION JOBS

THERE ARE AS MANY DIFFERENT JOBS IN animation as there are in cartooning. Animators are employed to make television shows as well as feature-length movies. In addition, animators work on video games and commercials.

Tweeners

Most animators start out in the field as in-betweeners or tweeners. Lead character animators draw the main cels (the images on celluloid), and tweeners generate the intermediate frames between the key scenes to ensure the smooth flow of the images. This is a very important part of the process. It fills in the gaps, completes the action, maintains consistency in the work, finishes sequences, and saves lead character animators time so they can work on other main cels. It is also an excellent way for young animators to learn the business.

Cleanup Artists

Cleanup artists put the finishing touches on many of the

drawings. While tweeners fill in the gaps, cleanup artists smooth out the rough drawings, paying attention to every last detail to make the drawings look as lifelike as possible.

Storyboard Artists

Nothing is done in animation without a storyboard artist. Walt Disney started the concept of creating a storyboard to plan out every shot in a movie before actually drawing it. This process helps maintain the continuity of the project.

Storyboard artists do mostly rough sketching. They arrange and rearrange the sketches on the drawing board until they find a flow that makes the storytelling work. Storyboard artists have to know the story that is being told thoroughly. They have to be interpreters of the work and understand how the story unfolds.

When the storyboard is complete, it becomes the scene--by-scene guide to what the finished work onscreen will look like. Storyboards are used in everything from feature-length movies, to short cartoons and commercials.

Layout Artists

Layout artists create the environment the characters in the production live in. It is the job of the layout artist to stage and set up each shot in the project. In this position, you have to pay careful attention to the composition of each scene. Layout artists do a great deal of research. If you hold this job, you have to be able to visualize the setting from various angles and perspectives. You must sense how a character will move in each setting. Knowledge of what a camera can do is essential. This job mirrors the work of a set designer for a movie, only in animation you are not limited by reality.

Background Animators

Background animators develop the backdrops for all the scenes in a production. For this job, you must have a solid understanding of the story and the characters, but you do your work for the characters without those characters actually in the scene. Once the background is completed, the characters are placed on top of it. This is another job in animation that calls for great visualization skills.

Effects Animators

Enormously patient and detail-oriented artists, called effects animators, add natural phenomena like lightning, fire and hail, and even the supernatural, to an animated feature. These important elements set the mood and establish the physical conditions and natural forces involved in the story that is being told.

Character Animator

One of the premier jobs at an animation studio is the character animator. Character animators are the major stars in the animation business. This job comes with many challenges and calls for a steady stream of new, creative, cutting-edge ideas. The goal of this job is to present something that has never been seen before, to set a new industry standard each time out. This job requires you to express your ideas clearly. It involves infusing each character with a unique personality. You bring to this job the ability to create characters that show emotion in their movements and facial expressions.

Director and Producer

Directors, art directors, and producers are all involved in animation as well, deciding on the direction of the project and making sure the whole effort comes together on time and on budget.

Vitally important to the entire animation process is teamwork. Animated productions are such massive undertakings that they can only be accomplished by a dedicated team, with each member acutely aware that the only way the job gets done is by all team members doing their parts well.

STORIES OF WORKING CARTOONISTS

I Am a Newspaper Cartoonist

"There are still many newspapers in the United States on both the daily and weekly level, and they like using witty, clever, and pertinent editorial cartoons. You can say so much with a cartoon that you just can't express in long-winded written editorials. People can get a chuckle from a cartoon by just taking a quick glance.

When people see a cartoon they like, they clip it out of the newspaper and slap it on a bulletin board or on the fridge. It is a great way for an illustrator to express a point of view and for others who agree with it to display that point of view. Today, editorial cartoons appear in other media as well, including many websites. Political cartoons are part of our country's heritage.

You have to have a talent for drawing to be a political cartoonist, but there are many other aspects to it as well. You have to have a great sense of humor, and the humor in your cartoons has to appeal to the average reader. The jokes have to keep on coming, day after day.

If you work for a daily newspaper and your editorial cartoons appear in the paper every day, getting a laugh out of people once a week or every few days just isn't good enough. You have got to be on target a good 95 percent of the time, or you lose the audience. Some people have a rather obscure sense of humor that most other folks just don't get. That doesn't work for political cartoonists. Everyone has to get the punch line in your work or you simply won't last very long in the business. People want to look at the cartoon and get a quick good laugh. Do not make them work to get it. The best thing for me is when I express a point of view in a cartoon and even someone who does not agree with me still gets a laugh.

The thing I really find amazing is how much you have to know to do this job. You have to have a broad-based liberal arts education. Knowing history is a must so you can stick in various historical figures in your cartoons. I love to throw past political figures or social activists into a cartoon about something happening today, and write a few succinct words about what they would probably say about what is happening. So you have to learn as much as you can about these giants of the past – Thomas Jefferson, Abe Lincoln, Susan B. Anthony – just to string together a few words about what they might think about a current issue.

You must know your current events, pop culture,

music, art, and politics, in order to get as many references as you can in your cartoons. You have to stay current, but at the same time be able to hearken back to the past to say, 'Here we go again.' You don't need many words, but you need the right ones. You have to choose your words carefully. The wrong words can kill the cartoon."

I Am a Comic Book Artist

"I illustrate and do some of the writing for comic books. I like being able to do some of the editorial work on the books, but I was hired for my artwork.

Today there are all kinds of comic books. The money is in doing work for the big comic book companies. Naturally, the mainstream titles like Superman and Batman are at the top, but it takes some time to work your way up to those titles. There is a chance that you can work on some lesser-known titles at these mainstream comic book publishers and still make a good and steady salary. There are drawbacks to working for mainstream publishers, and one of them is that you usually do not own the rights to your work, even if you create a character from scratch.

I do a great deal of work for alternative comics. These are rather unconventional titles that stray from the mainstream super hero comics. Alternative comics come in a number of genres and cover a variety of topics. Some cartoonists both illustrate and write these comics, while other alternative comics are produced by an artist/writer team.

When it comes to alternative comics, there is a great deal of creative freedom for both the artists and writers. The publisher is not deciding on the storyline or even the direction of the story, as is often the case in mainstream comics. The way the story goes is your choice.

The alternative comics market can be rather unstable. These comics are usually produced by much smaller publishers who do not have the same distribution networks as mainstream publishers, and they don't have as much money to spend. On the other hand, you usually can keep the rights to your work, and you have creative control of your characters.

The release schedules for alternative comics may be sporadic, which means fans do not know exactly when the next issue is coming out, and that can hurt sales a bit. There is always the possibility of the publisher going out of business, or the comic being dropped from the line because there isn't a big enough fan following. For many cartoonists, part of the challenge of the alternative comics market is getting their characters known to a wide audience.

I find that most people working in alternative comics do it for the love of the work, because the money is not always there. Many alternative comic book artists also have mainstream jobs, like illustrating greeting cards, advertisements, or even drawing illustrations or political cartoons for newspapers and magazines. It allows them to make a steady income while nurturing a career in comic books."

I Am a Computer Animator

"I work in feature films. Even though most animation today is done on computers, I believe you need to have excellent drawing skills to succeed in this field.

Most animators I work with like to make rough drawings on paper before they start working on the computer. I have always done this. It gives me a visual to work from and allows the work to take shape. I am a firm believer that these initial hand-drawn sketches are an important part of the process, so you have to be able to draw well.

Even before you get to the initial drawing stage, you have to take the time to really get into the script. I read it two or three times. Then, I study the storyboards for the film. I also listen to the recorded dialogue that has been made for the movie. I really want to get to know the story that is being told and understand every nuance. Not only that, I want to get to know the characters. That is how I can bring them to life on the screen.

Even though they are not human actors, when we get done with a film, we want moviegoers to feel like they were watching living, breathing actors on that screen. We want those characters to show emotions, just like humans. It is part of the magic.

By the time I am ready to sit down and draw, I feel like I'm a lawyer going into court for a big case. I know everything there is to know about what I am working on. I don't want any surprises. It is all plotted out in my head.

I work with a team, and we all have to prepare this way. Animated films require an enormous amount of work. Don't forget that in an animated film, the animators are responsible for every move that is made on the screen. The whole flow of the film is up to you. Animators must completely understand what the scriptwriters are trying to convey and get that point across. You do that with every movement the characters make. You do it with facial expressions and gestures. You do that with the scenery. Everything has to look and feel real.

Doing all this work on computers means that you need excellent technical skills, in addition to creative talent. You have to be facile with the software you are using. You want to use the latest technology to create the 'wow' factor in every movie you make. That is what keeps fans coming back to the movie theaters, and that's what keeps me coming into work every day. What can we do today, that we couldn't do yesterday?"

PERSONAL QUALITIES

THE MOST IMPORTANT THING YOU HAVE to be able to do is draw well. Though much is done on computers when it comes to animation, employers will want to know that you can draw, and they want to see proof of it.

When it comes to drawing, your work has to be outstanding on many levels. Many art school students can draw very well if they have a model in front of them. Animators and cartoonists usually draw freehand, without any models or points of reference – to create something totally new. This is what distinguishes true talent.

If you know how to draw, you will always be able to find a job in some part of this career field – whether it is in advertising, comic strips, or movie animation. Your drawing talent gives you the versatility you need to succeed in this business.

You must actively love to draw. This means your parents had to pry a pencil out of your hand ever since you were five or six years old. You are in this line of work for the pure joy of creating something new, exhilarating, and fresh. Creativity is a number-one priority in this field.

Finding a way to improve your work every time you draw something has to be a priority. Also, having a great deal of confidence in your talent, and being your own toughest critic are essential. You can never be satisfied because being the best means pushing the envelope with each new idea you develop.

There are many candidates eager to enter the field of animation and cartooning, so persistence and an intense desire to succeed will help you stand out. You might be discouraged and feel like giving up after several rejections. You must believe in yourself enough to keep going. This is similar to actors going on auditions. You continue to try until you succeed, working to perfect your talent along the way.

Something often overlooked is writing ability. Oftentimes, artists are called on to fill in the blanks when it comes to story line, so it is worthwhile to develop your writing skills. Cartoonists often write the words to go along with their drawings, so being able to turn a phrase is useful. Having a sense of humor always helps in coming up with the double entendres and rapid-fire punch lines that make people respond to cartoons.

Being very aware of how people think and feel will help you deliver work that resonates with readers and that builds a following. Keeping up with current events and what is happening in the world around you is important. Animated television shows are current and edgy. For feature-length movies, animators have to know what viewers will relate to. These films, even if they are age-old fables, always have a few lines that fit right in with life today.

ATTRACTIVE FEATURES

YOU WILL HAVE A CHANCE TO USE your creativity all the time! Whether you are working on your own idea or putting the finishing touches on someone else's, you are using your talent to do something that relatively few people can, and earning your living at it.

Political and editorial cartoonists, as well as those who draw humorous comics, typically have relatively free rein over their work. You usually have a job at a newspaper, magazine, or with a company that distributes your work. More often than not, your employer shares your point of view.

You are able to express yourself or a particular opinion through your drawings and the illustrated characters you bring to the fore. You can give those characters their own personalities. If you get a gig where your drawings appear on a regular basis, you can develop a style of drawing and a slant on the issues of the day that are uniquely your own. You have a platform, and possibly a great deal of influence.

That is not true just for political cartoonists. Comic strips like Charles Schultz's Peanuts can take on a life of their own, going from newspapers to television, books, and many other marketing tie-ins. You have a chance to produce a character that can become part of the fabric of a community or as, in the case of the Peanuts comic strip and many others, the whole country. Likewise, successful animators with a few hits on their résumé can pretty much take their characters in any direction they want, as long as the public keeps paying to see them.

As a cartoonist or animator, you use your imagination in your work every day, and you can develop characters based on your own life experiences. The popular syndicated comic strip Family Circus, by cartoonist Bill Keane, was based on Keane's own family members.

Your work can become extremely well known, be seen everywhere, be the latest sensation and the talk of the town, and you can still live in relative anonymity, if you choose. It is not your face people are seeing, not you they are talking about. You have the satisfaction of being successful, getting the financial compensation to go along with that, see the public admiration for characters you created, have ongoing work and a chance to develop new projects – and still maintain your privacy. Not a bad deal, Charlie Brown.

Most animators work in a team atmosphere, which means the weight of an entire project does not fall on one person. If you need help or want to bounce some ideas off someone, there is a member of the team around who has a total understanding of what the job is all about and can offer thoughts and ideas to help you get over some of the rough spots.

If you work on a freelance basis – and many cartoonists and animators do – you can set your own hours and work at your convenience. That does not mean you will not work hard, you just will not be tied down to a set daily schedule. The only catch is you still have to meet your deadlines.

UNATTRACTIVE FEATURES

ANIMATION AND CARTOONING ARE difficult fields to break into. You cannot be discouraged easily and you have to continue to go after the job you want. You must be able to deal with rejection. You may submit work and have it rejected several times. It does not matter how good you feel the work is, those who are employing you have to like it as well, and if they do not, you might have to start from scratch.

You may be working on one project for quite some time until everyone involved in it agrees on the drawings to use. For a creative person, this approval process may be extremely frustrating.

When you first enter the business, the pay is low and the hours are long. The long hours usually don't bring the benefit of any overtime pay.

Tight deadlines may force you to work nights, weekends, and holidays. Deadlines will control a great deal of your life. You will have to be able to work your everyday life around deadlines that come up suddenly.

Early on in your career, you will probably spend most of your time working on fleshing out someone else's ideas. It could be years before you get a chance to work on your own ideas. Your suggestions may be overlooked or ignored. You will have to be patient in order to get your chance to bring your own ideas to life. You will never know when that chance will come along, but you will have to be ready when it does.

You will have to deal with the highs and lows of the business. This is difficult because these are usually out of your control. For instance, newspapers and print magazines are declining in number at this time. That is bad news for those who draw comic strips and political cartoons for the print media. Comic strips and political cartoons have a loyal fan base, and they will always be around in one form or another. Many newspapers include their comic strips and cartoons in their online versions.

Animation is booming right now, after going through a lull in the 1970s and 1980s. No one knows how long that boom will last. Animated characters, like movie stars, have a limited shelf life. The public can be fickle. After loving one character for a certain period, they turn their attention to the next best thing. You have to be ready to move on and create something new.

Coping with a creative block is never easy. Artists, like writers, get blocks, and learning how to work through them may cause you trouble. Unfortunately, these dry spells, where you lack creative motivation and fresh ideas, come without warning and with deadlines looming. The best in the business stay at the top by knowing how to break out of these slumps.

EDUCATION AND TRAINING

IT IS ALWAYS A DIFFICULT DECISION whether to pursue formal education after high school at an art school or in a college that offers art classes but not concentrated programs in art. There is no right or wrong answer. It is a good idea to look into both and see which program suits you and your goals better.

Many cartoonists seek to supplement their art education with journalism courses or broad-based liberal arts courses. That is because the work of most cartoonists is based on a variety of subjects, and being exposed to those topics in literature, history, political science, psychology, and sociology courses helps in their work.

One day you might be doing a drawing on poverty in America, and the next day it can be something dealing with a political stalemate in the US Congress. To draw realistically and make cartoons that are relevant, it helps to have a working knowledge and some insight into politics and culture.

A well-rounded education also gives you more options. If you find you do not really like cartooning as a full-time career, you have skills in other fields. If you want to start out in another field and do cartooning on the side, you also have that option.

A wide-ranging education helps in animation as well, but you need to find a course of study that also provides you with cutting-edge technical skills. You will have to learn how to blend your artistic and creative talent on paper with the computer wizardry that is taking animation to new levels every day.

The School for the Visual Arts (SVA) in New York City is considered one of the top colleges for visual arts in the nation. The school does offer undergraduate degrees, and while the curriculum is art-specific, it includes general studies in the humanities and sciences. Degrees are awarded in cartooning, illustration, animation, computer animation, fine arts, and many other art-related fields. Graduate degrees are available in a number of specialties.

Another outstanding art school is Pratt Institute in New York City. This college has a varied curriculum that includes courses on illustration and animation, with an array of other art and design programs, as well as liberal arts, math, and science.

Savannah College of Art and Design, with campuses in both Savannah and Atlanta, Georgia, is another well-known college that emphasizes the arts, but requires students to take liberal arts classes as well, in order to earn an undergraduate degree. The college has courses in all the fine arts, as well as illustration, animation, comic strips, and interactive video-game development. The school hosts many events to promote the arts and the work of its students, including an annual film festival.

Illustration and animation are among the core programs at the Academy of Art University in San Francisco. The school has been teaching art and design since 1929. With 18 degree and certificate programs, including Bachelor of Fine Arts and Master of Fine Arts, the academy has helped launch the careers of many young artists.

Ball State University in Muncie, Indiana has a growing animation program that prepares students to work in films, television, video games, advertising, and architectural rendering. The school now offers a Master of Fine Arts degree in animation, to go along with its undergraduate degrees in the subject.

Bowling Green University in Ohio has an in-depth program for students who want to enter the field of computer animation. Part of the college's Digital Arts Division of the School of Art, the animation program teaches students to use technology to push the limits of their creativity.

Some of the other major universities with animation programs include University of Washington in Seattle, University of Utah in Salt Lake City, University of Massachusetts in Amherst, San Jose State University in California, and New York University in New York City.

The Center for Cartoon Studies in White River Junction, Vermont offers a two-year program that focuses strictly on comic art. Someone with an undergraduate degree from another college can get a Master of Fine Arts degree from the school. Those who do not have an undergraduate degree can get a certificate in cartooning from the school. The Center for Cartoon Studies, however, does not offer undergraduate degrees. The school is for students who want dedicated career training in the field of graphic novels and comic books.

Another art school that has distinguished itself nationwide is the Joe Kubert School of Cartoon and Graphic Arts in Dover, New Jersey. Founded by the well-known comic book artist Joe Kubert, this three-year technical school is all about comic book art. Teachers at the school are full-time professionals in the comic book industry. They give hands-on advice to students about what they need to learn to break into and succeed in the competitive business of cartoon art.

Prospective students are usually required to submit a portfolio for review before being accepted in a cartooning or animation program at many colleges and art schools.

EARNINGS

SALARIES VARY GREATLY IN CARTOONING and animation. The range goes all the way from starving artist to six-figure annual earnings. Many cartoonists work on a freelance basis, and they are usually paid per project. Those fees can range from $50 to $1,000 or more per drawing.

Newspapers and magazines often have cartoonists on staff to draw everything from political cartoons to illustrations for features and news stories. The salary range for these jobs goes anywhere from $30,000 to $60,000, and possibly more if it is a well-known publication.

Syndicated cartoonists can make as much as $100,000 a year, depending on how many newspapers nationwide publish their work. For some very popular newspaper comic strips, tie-in marketing boosts the cartoonist's income, through sales of merchandise like books, T-shirts and coffee mugs based on the characters. The same is true for comic book artists. They can earn from $30,000 a year, for work done on lesser-known comic book titles, to nearly $200,000 for work on a well-known series, like Spider-Man or The Hulk.

There are many different jobs in animation, and working your way through the ranks brings increases in earnings. Major animation studios pay more than smaller ones, especially the small ones that are just starting out and are looking for that first big hit. Tweeners start out with an annual salary of about $25,000, and through the years can see increases up to $45,000. Other average yearly salaries in animation include color stylist, $65,000; background painters, $90,000; effects animator, $100,000; character animator, $125,000; art director, $150,000; and producer, $200,000.

OPPORTUNITIES

THE OPPORTUNITIES AVAILABLE THESE days for cartoonists differ from those for animators. Anyone who reads a newspaper realizes that comic strips are still out there. So are political cartoons and drawings in magazines. Illustrations continue to appear on greeting cards and calendars.

However, there are fewer openings in the print media for cartoonists than there are in animation. Nevertheless, people love their Sunday funnies, and newspaper syndicates are always looking for comic strips that express an edgy point of view of the world. It is a matter of supply and demand: fewer newspapers means it is tougher to break into the business.

Even with less expansion of print media, cartoon art seems to be popping up everywhere you look. That is because newspapers and magazines are not the only outlet for cartoonists. An ever-increasing number of manufacturers are looking for catchy, original characters and logos to use on labels and packaging to help sell products. Cartoonists create those logos and characters. The rich tradition of Tony the Tiger and Charlie the Tuna is alive and well and still attracts people to a product on the shelf.

Comic books, while part of the print industry, are doing well in the computer age. In fact, loyal fans continue to buy, read, and collect comic books, even though prices have gone up. That segment of print media seems to be surging and holds great promise for cartoonists.

The field of animation is booming at the moment, and there are no signs of it letting up any time soon. One of the big growth areas for animators is computer games. These games are so popular that companies cannot put them out fast enough. Entire companies have sprung up dedicated to issuing the latest and hottest computer games, and that requires the work of many extremely gifted animators.

Naturally, animation goes far beyond computer games. It has actually changed the culture of television. Situation comedies, which for decades featured human actors, have been replaced in some time slots by animated cartoon series. These series tackle serious subjects in a kooky offbeat style. A leading example is the FOX Network's series *The Simpsons,* which debuted to a doubting audience in 1989 and has aired ever since. Rival networks have followed suit, developing other animated series for adult audiences, like *South Park* and *Family Guy*. This activity is in addition to cartoon shows for children on Saturday mornings and after school on weekdays. There are numerous opportunities for animators to develop work for entire cable networks devoted exclusively to cartoons. Making commercials is also an excellent way for animators to break into the business and can prove to be a fruitful career.

Feature-length animated films are more popular than ever, especially with the addition of 3-D. While many of these animated feature-length films go to the big screen, sequels sometimes go right to DVD, creating a long afterlife for spinoffs of these popular films and more work for animators.

GETTING STARTED

ANIMATION AND CARTOONING ARE fields where you really have to prove yourself in order to move up. Most people just starting out in this field will have to get some work experience before advancing. That does not mean you will not be able to break into the field; it just means that you will probably start in an entry-level position.

A strong portfolio is an important asset when you are looking for a job in animation and cartooning. Many artists spend a great deal of time building that portfolio. One way to do that is to take on freelance jobs while you are still in school. There are many magazines, newspapers, and advertising agencies that need an occasional job done here and there, and that is just the type of work that can help you fill out your portfolio.

Do not turn down nonpaying gigs. We all want to be paid for our work, but in the very competitive field of cartooning, sometimes you have to do some drawing gratis in order to get your work seen, and the word out there that you are available.

There are many nonprofit organizations that would be more than happy to have you volunteer to illustrate their brochures, newsletters, and posters, which, in turn, gives you a platform for your work. Be sure to request an illustration credit for any work you do – especially work for free.

Consider doing work on spec. This means you submit the completed work, and only if it is accepted do you get paid. This may turn out to be a situation where you spend time on a project for little or no money, but it may be an opportunity to get some good exposure. When you are doing work on spec, it is important to understand all the ground rules from the outset, and to try to learn as much as you can about the other people involved in the project. Try to get a contract for jobs done on spec. The contract should spell out what you will be paid if the work is accepted, and how long those who are buying it are entitled to use it. Work done on spec may also be rejected, in which case you are paid nothing. It is a chance you take, but not an uncommon practice in this field.

Few people going into animation find full-time work immediately. Consider taking a part-time job at the drawing board, not only for the work experience but to get your name around in the industry.

There are numerous internships in animation and cartooning available these days, some with large studios. These openings should not be overlooked. Some of the internships are paid positions. Many are not, but consider the contacts you can make and the experience you can get. Think of it as a tryout for both the studio and you. This could work into a part-time or a full-time job, and it also gives you a chance to get a foot in the door and see what it is like to work in this field.

ASSOCIATIONS

■ **Society of Illustrators**
www.societyillustrators.org

■ **National Cartoonists Society**
www.reuben.org

■ **Association of American Editorial Cartoonists (AAEC)**
http://editorialcartoonists.com

■ **Comic Art Professional Society**
www.capscentral.org

■ **Graphic Artist Guild**
www.graphicartistsguild.org

■ **Association Internationale du Film d'Animation (France)**
www.ASIFA.org

■ **International Animated Film Association (USA)**
http://ASIFA.net

PERIODICALS

■ **Cartoon Brew**

■ **The Artist's Magazine**

■ **Animation Magazine**

- AnimationWorld Magazine
- Animation Journal
- The Comics Journal
- The New Yorker

WEBSITES

- Charles M. Schulz Museum & Research Center
www.schulzmuseum.org

- San Diego Comic-Con International
www.comic-con.org

- Museum of Comic and Cartoon Art (MoCCA)
www.moccany.org

- The Political Cartoon Society
www.politicalcartoon.co.uk

- Ohio State University Cartoon Library & Museum
http://cartoons.osu.edu

- Cartoon Art Museum–San Francisco
http://cartoonart.org

- Animation Library
www.animationlibrary.com

- Walt Disney Animation Studios
www.disneyanimation.com

- Pixar Animation Studios
www.pixar.com